DAVID MILLER
SOME OTHER SHADOWS

Newton-le-Willows

Published in the United Kingdom in 2022
by The Knives Forks And Spoons Press,
51 Pipit Avenue,
Newton-le-Willows,
Merseyside,
WA12 9RG.

ISBN 978-1-912211-92-0

Acknowledgements:

Arcane Libraries appeared as a very limited broadsheet edition from Kater Murr's Press.

Gospel Songs appeared on *otoliths* (online journal).

Vitruvian Shadows appeared in a very limited edition chapbook from The Red Ceilings Press.

Deliverance was another very limited edition from Kater Murr's Press. God bless the Cat.

The Death of a Giraffe and other poems was published as part of *hardPressed Dual Poets: Reader Two*, hardPressed Poetry.

Supported using public funding by
ARTS COUNCIL ENGLAND

LOTTERY FUNDED

For Dodo, with love

Contents

ARCANE LIBRARIES

I went to libraries
arcane libraries

I went to bookshops
arcane bookshops

by subterranean routes
mostly at night

but not any more

I hunger I thirst
my heart my soul my spirit

the doors
ajar

the gates
open

let alone locked

& never otherwise

GOSPEL SONGS

something bronze
or glass

or else sand

lightning & fire
strike

musicians
in strange places

strange?
there were back streets

& odd structures

buildings
where they sang

& played
& where

they prayed

& I
wished to join them

a climate
of miracles

healing
laying on of hands

into wholeness

in stories ...

stories
yes

&
later at least

in songs

or
a climate

of suspicion

a climate
of denial

a hand
or hands

hoping for
iron & steel

touching synthetics

touching tiles
at best

grasping
cardboard

grabbing at
snow ice sleet rain

belief
dwells

with
doubt

faith
dwells

with un-
certainty

uncertainty
dwells

with
belief

doubt
dwells

with
faith

David Miller

a rain
of sparrows

a rain
of swifts

a rain
of starlings

a reign
of quantity

rippled
glass

so cold
yes

cold

elsewhere
heat haze

horizons
blurred

harried

she hid her face
(tears)

I drank wine

elsewhere
the child

thus
& thus

start from nothing
or as close to nothing

as possible

& call it purity
as a starting point

for an exception

a new beginning
from the old

or oldest

children slaughtered
in moonlight & sunlight

an escape on an ass

in moonlight
& sunlight

& moonlight

oldest
or

rather

some-
thing

other

(not
Egyptian

or
Babylonian)

… &
I wished to join them

who?
those I mean who were made whole

were made whole?

whose demons had been driven from them
who were blind & now could see

– such as we've heard & heard! & to what purpose?

ah who were rendered limpid
rendered at least but more

limpid? yes in uncertainty

if rendered
then somehow whole

if whole
then somehow rendered

wood & nails
flesh & blood

the given?
the basic?

& the spirit
leaving the body

to be

otherwise
embodied

there was a road

there was a room
there was a supper

there was bread
there was wine

there was a tomb
there was a rock

there were wounds
there was a road

who was it
who wept?

I drank wine
but who wept?

& who sang?

IMPLICATIONS

could the stones cry out weep bleed said & as should

& the stones seams
in rocks red wine or white white flames

trees blood the chanter plays the bloody fields
drops over a face blood drops

on rocks on stone
red blue yellow green

as

striated

striated striated striated striated striated striated striated
striated striated striated striated striated striated striated
striated striated striated striated striated striated striated
striated striated striated striated striated striated striated
striated striated striated striated striated striated striated
striated striated striated striated striated striated striated

striated

& university buildings
where I lost myself

degrees taken not taken

night
somehow always night

night & buses back

to somewhere

so I remember
deaths

no I can't remember I was exempt
others went I didn't

went to fight & kill & die

what casualties there were
in those bloody fields

not just deaths
but grievous injuries

that would sicken the soul

& I don't remember
but I would

stri-
at-

ed
stone

blood

I

not that the blood
is the soul

certainly not the spirit

nor even the body

but tell that to the fields

it's now more & more
that I do look back

on those neon-lit
corridors &

lamppost-lit
courtyards

in otherwise
darkness

– having taught
& been taught

& having thought once
I would not reach 20

because of conscription
& war

& having now turned 70
having taught

& been taught

dreams take me mostly into night
but it was mostly daytime

when I studied & then taught

but darkness
& artificial light

override
overrule

beheadings
& other deaths

& injuries
in battle

*who killed
cock robin?*

I
said the sparrow

but the two
tomcats

who came knocking
at my door

in the depths of night
only knocked me down

unlike the knights
who jousted

who tested
who killed

& who pursued
the quest

never now or
drawing while sitting

further now
drawing

standing while drawing
kneeling while drawing

in the courtyard
of

abutted
later waters

drawing while running
yet

skies
yet you here there

to acquire wings
& drawing while gliding

the last bus had left for the night
about

abutted

my family doctor lied
to help me survive

I can say it now
now that he's long dead

splashed
those strange walls

David Miller

the out-of-place minaret
some eccentric erected

– I wanted to live there

& then the old walls
some painted in odd colours

some with the paint peeling
or plaster cracked

1960s South Melbourne
"shabby genteel"

my doctor's surgery

"shabby genteel"
when not working class

& then the public gardens

the doorbell chimes
during the night

there's nobody there

rain
& stone underfoot

the soul's
active

when the body's
inert

sees when
the body's

blind
lives when

the body's
dead

I

blood

stone

if

the cold's
a bond

it's not one
I'd bet on

for long

memory most prized
amongst mortals

give me water then cold water
yes cold water to drink

not from the spring
by the cypress

the cypress to the left
not from there

into milk

or into fields
after streets

& roads
the bus back

to somewhere
late at night

getting off at the wrong stop
a wall

David Miller

the implications

the bloody fields

the spring on the left
by the white cypress

the other spring
flowing forth with cold water

THE GOLD SHAPE

the gold shape
almost

an absence

the absence

almost
a

gold
shape

gold or
golden?

gold
or almost?

the gold shape
an absence

the absence
a gold shape

almost
an absence?

or
an

absence?

almost?

almost
gold

then

almost
absence

an absence
or an echo

shape
absence

echo

a circle
a circle behind

a person
a person's head

a person
within a circle

a person

a gold house

a tiny
gold house

a person
so very thin

not starved
– attenuated

yes elongated
unearthly

David Miller

the stairs
or lift

to his place
after back streets

somehow
always late at night

sometimes
he was alive

sometimes dead
never

with a halo
or within

a circle

a penumbra
no never

in my dreams of him
yet a penumbra?

what surrounds
& what says

what says?
a text says

says something

that which surrounds
& which speaks

& the text?

woven of gold
or so it seemed

& the tiny
house

constructed
of gold

woven
or

constructed

the gold
the rain

the memories
the dreams

the visions

woven
constructed

remembered
dreamt

envisioned

"not into anything gold
or even golden

neither woven
nor constructed"

did he say?

yes he said
as he turned

to leave

the reflections
the echoes

said otherwise

no matter
the poverty

of his flat
no matter

his eviction
no matter

his poems
destroyed

oh turned to rubbish

iron rings
an echo

an echo of gold

iron rings
formed

into an echo

constructed
or woven

a life
or lives

the living
the dead

we live
we die

woven
or constructed

a tiny
gold house

an elongated
figure

the lift
to your flat

sometimes
I'd be there

sometimes
you'd be there

& I'd arrive

sometimes
no one would answer

when I rang the bell
or sometimes

it was a stranger
ah who didn't even know you

the constellations

the harlequin

the juggler

the rings

the window

did it seem tiny?
or even gold?

when I visited?
when I stayed?

it was tiny
it was gold

you were elongated
though tiny

within

tiny ah so tiny
no not at all

you weren't
at my wedding

but that isn't

tiny ah so tiny no
no not at all

that you died

tiny ah so tiny no
you were a great friend

& a poet whose writings
were destroyed

almost entirely

"I have a project now"
if a glass held

by the stem

"to see
if there are any

stars in the sky"

then a full glass
of yellow wine

then can I conjure?
can I conjure rings?

can I juggle?
if so

how many juggling balls
can I sustain?

if a glass wall

the harlequin

the juggler

the artist

the film-maker

the musician

the composer

the storyteller

the novelist

the playwright

the poet

the philosopher

the mystic

the saint

the philosopher?

possibly

if
a gold shape

then
an absence

or almost
an absence

& a poet

& a lift
or else stairs

to a flat
where once

I visited

a harlequin
a juggler

a gold shape
an absence

a ring
a set of rings

a constellation
or a

bird table
with blackbirds

crows
pigeons

starlings
magpies

& the poet
has come to the table

he's dead
of course

elongated

almost
absence

VITRUVIAN
SHADOWS

& if so then yes ah yes
yes *there will be a space*

yes *to the right* to the right
yes silver against glass

it commands a view of the forum
& water of course

the harbour yes the harbour
a tree a tree branch

trees painted white half way
against blue always blue

the dignity of the whole
ah the sands

the arcades ... ah yes
& drunkenness

because its water is said to be death-dealing

David Miller

a dance without dancers
or else dancers

without
a dance

a much wider space for the walk round the cella
the sands the arcades

her face painted in patterns
all over

there is a water those who taste of which
immediately fall lifeless

close by this fount there is a tree
with crimson flowers

a portrait in dream
in black grey blue

& white
& the white painted trees

& the ever blue water
out of place

& elsewhere
the exit I took from the station proved the wrong one I was lost

more lost than might be imagined
ramps obstacles ramps & obstacles

small sets of apartments
are built both right & left

with front doors of their own
& an eidolon at the door

down the stone steps
as if to an underground urinal

but to a venue for experimental music
nothing derogatory a space that's suitable

without urinals
let bronze vessels be made

so fashioned that when touched

they may produce with one another
the notes of the fourth the fifth & so on up to the double octave

the drops of rain
there was a bar I asked for wine

– silence at the end of a film showing
& then:

"you have to realise that what you're doing
has nothing to do with art"

ah so be it though they thought otherwise
psychodrama yes

or that was what was said
so wake up to the life the life that you're living

someone's life at least
a cold blue stellar light

dark blue
ah to run run quickly down enormous stone staircases

when you're small
past magnificent fountains splashing

the space is there it's viable the life
so yes wake up to it missing trains how confused

elsewhere always elsewhere? elsewhere
the hanging floors

I met him by chance on the street
"come for a meal" he said yes always

I replied that our friend was waiting at my place
the rain the rain the rain the rain yes the rain

he'd never go out in the rain if ... if? yes if he could go another time
the arcades Classical? ah ersatz Classical buildings elsewhere

coffee bars wine bars arcades where we met
elsewhere Classical buildings out of time not timeless decadent

& the poets obeyed the politics
some some not all but some someone

the winds are witnesses
deaths murders tortures anyway you say it

there are some cold springs
that have a bad smell & taste

if so then so
then a pen to write

I did miss trains I was confused yes
voice is a flowing breath of air

& to say to witness to write
& I'd give it all for a great jazz bass solo I admit

Cecil McBee or Ron Carter
Charlie Haden or Scott LaFaro

if so then so ah yes
the trains ran

what would I give? not lives
not the possibility of not suffering not suffering suffering

because you're a Jew or a Christian or gay
or Romany or black or female or else or other

there or elsewhere
I plead & then refuse to plead & then plead & still plead despite all rhetoric

autism
that too

archival
ah archival

psychodrama or trance it could be yes
& so many times I would take a bus there on the off chance dear friend

desolate
the smallest birds the ones I loved & still love best

& if so then yes
yes of course it does follow

a seller of salt he said
"would you say this was the birth of modernism?" no

a strange man & a stranger "no" I said
he meant Vitruvius I meant Machiavelli

then there are springs in which wine seems to be mingled
a clod of good yellow ochre is heated on a fire

it is then quenched in vinegar
the result is a purple colour

ink spilled stained painted in dots in stripes
smearing & overpainting yes

& lines drawn in pencil

he died
you & I married

so also a pearl
a pearl that dies and marries? dies & marries

the rules of symmetry & proportion
man's intelligence is made keener by warm air

& duller by cold
& then stopped by screens palms faces in dreams

life & afterlife yes
rooms for grain & yes other rooms

David Miller

columbaria yes dovecotes
the scheme of dentils

they set sail in trance
out to disaster

if there were waves
they'd sail to disaster

the hospital
the museum

I'd seen bodies bodies? no not bodies people yes & yes also bodies
I'd seen paintings & sculptures & prints assemblages & collages

the waters
the still waters

& the split & broken columns

the blackbird splashes frenetically bathing in the bird bath
yes & so said:

flickering or glimmering
glistening or brimming

& I moved to the country
& if so then so

as soon as common oak boards get damp
they warp & cause cracks in floors

the broken stone with its bedding

David Miller

& the bus from Rome to Weymouth
wouldn't leave for five hours

I had to ditch belongings student papers
due for marking not a priority

but were my papers in order & where
could I find somewhere to eat & somewhere

to piss & shit it was Fascist Italy
& were my papers indeed in order?

& on the ferry would my money
provide for food & drink & a berth?

– a dream of course

the destroyer called the raven
or by others the crane

they demolished the entire redoubt
& who said history is a nightmare we try to wake from?

DEATH OF A GIRAFFE

and other poems

Starting from a Photograph by Diane Arbus

I encountered her in the park, a tough-looking young woman smoking a cigar; she had cropped blonde hair, and the glazed eyes of a drug addict: or so it seemed. She obligingly posed for my camera; but she still scared the shit out of me.

Oblique.

"No, I turned myself in," she said; "I didn't want it hanging over me at Christmas. What was it about? – just getting into an argument with some fucking idiot."

Direct: you might say so; in some respects. Not so much face-to-face: more face-at-face.

A cutpurse? Possibly. Two shadows to one person, simultaneously thrown by a single sun.

Coming across an elderly woman harassed by an Alsatian dog, she punched the animal in the face.

Urban and industrial panoramas squeezed and further squeezed: elongated buildings (silos; tenements; high-rise hotels), pushed towards and against each other. Wire fences. Barbed.

Where she lives:

There's a window box, with geraniums; a toy bird, singing; a spider in the bathroom; a cracked wine glass. And a yellow-ochre sky in view.

She encountered a scholar; a scholar lost to himself. A scholar of what? he wondered.

She might lift her hand or not, smoke or not, turn or not, pose or not, leave the park and re-enter it, light a cigar, pose and then pose again. She might pursue herself, flee herself, pass herself and continue or come back.

"We may eat cubs if we think they were sired by another male, but we're not barbarians," said a lion in her dream.

She pursues, and is pursued.

In soldierly perspective. Towers; fortifications: open to the corporeal eye, via the mind's eye. *Measured outlines, like footprints, have no point of view.*

A star, six-pointed, formed the top of the tower, poised at the heavens; echoed in shape by surrounding walls.

Long range missiles, suicide aircraft strikes. Then artillery fire.

Walls, in ruins: rubble.

Her form ebbs and flows, strengthens and fades.

Landscapes withered, bleached, blasted: etiolated here, burnt and blackened there.

Black. A red edge. Fire. Stone; rocks.

Echo.

Or, finally, nothing to echo.

Deliverance

Forests were being devastated by bush fires, the worst for a very long time, with animals losing their homes and in many cases their lives. Humans died, as well, but the main victims were such as koalas, kangaroos, wombats, possums ...

Des and Billy decided to do something to help. Quite ordinary young men, to most intents and purposes, they felt sorry for the koalas, especially, and thought they could rescue at least a few of them. These marsupials are likely to just climb higher up their trees, where they'll perish, or if on the ground they'll be confused and frightened by the fire and smoke and not know what to do.

Des and Billy also liked a little adventure, and rescuing koalas seemed at least as good as any other.

So they took Billy's station wagon and drove to where the nearest trees were burning. They both listened to loud rock music through their headphones, but Billy's eyes were on the road and Des' on the trees and ground.

They spotted their first koala, climbing a gum tree, and stopped the car and hurried over. Des flung his jacket over the koala and they both grabbed hold of it and carried it back to the car. It struggled, but once it was sitting on the back seat it seemed to relax, oddly enough.

"Aw, he's enjoying the view!" exclaimed Des, and he and Billy gave each other a high-five.

Soon there were three koalas sitting in the back, and all of them did, indeed, seem to be looking at the view.

"There's a gum tree," said one koala, looking out the window, "and there's another one ... and another ... "

"Yeah, we've been looking at them as well. Aw, damn, there's a dead 'roo. That's sad!" said the second koala.

"Yeah, I tend to like 'roos", said the third. "Pity."

"So where are you guys from?"

"Aw, down the road a bit."

"Me, too."

"Me, too."

"Funny we've never met before."

"Yeah."

"And what a way to meet!"

"You said it, mate."

"Yeah, look at that fire and smoke! God, it's awful."

"Those two guys in front, listening to that din … "

"Yeah?"

"Good thing we rescued them in time!"

"That's right, sport!"

"Never a truer word!"

Clarinet

A clarinettist plays and dreams ... dreams and plays: what else should he (or she) do?

Until a tiny spider crawled its way into the clarinet and made its home there, chewing the pad beneath a key and also laying its eggs.

The bottom notes, most dearly prized, rendered unplayable.

Then he (or she) could only dream.

David Miller

Bali, 1930s/40s

long into the night
gamelan music sounding
to cheer the prisoner
keeping him company
painter photographer
homosexual
predator?
interned on the island

　　　...

riding in carriages
pulled by the poor
lady anthropologist
's breakdown
trance her subject
all to a point of no
return

　　　...

and his death at sea
after another internment
and deportation
ghostly repetitions
under moonlight
ordinary and monstrous

East London, 1975

his long hair pulled
and stones and glass
thrown by children
at the young stranger
in the street at night

    ...

clutching his clarinet case
for dear life

David Miller

Bushfires (I)

Fires set

then sit

then run

Bushfires (II)

— My ear fur and paws
your beak and feathers

burnt

David Miller

Bushfires (III)

The animals turn back
as the smoke thickens

Death of a Giraffe

Blood spurts from the long neck
and the long legs give way

David Miller

Air Rifle

A shot to its eye
a shot to its side

(yet the cat may live)

The Pencil of Nature
(after Fox Talbot)

These are the sun-pictures themselves
and not
en-
grav-
ings
in im-
itation

David Miller

Dew Still There?

Dew still there?
or else rain
earlier in the day:
after putting out food
for the birds
slippers and trouser ends soaked

Honeycomb, waffles, pancakes with syrup. Strong coffee with milk.

A Barque. Or a Catafalque

A barque. Or a catafalque.

From exile and into exile: we are born, live and die, exilic.

And strive to be ethical.

— That day promised much; but the sky and the sea darkened ... and then all was lost.

A lock of ash-blonde hair.

David Miller

(for Robinson Jeffers)

your hand writes
my hand writes

ghost hand writes

In

in
the

blue

blue

blue

David Miller

Fields of Ash

ash	ash	ash	ash
sadism	ash	ash	ash
murder	ash	ash	ash
genocide	ash	ash	ash

Notes

Implications:

'the soul's/ active ... ' is adapted from a sentence ascribed (spuriously) to Hippōn of Samos, which I found in Kathleen Freeman's *Ancilla to the Pre-Socratic Philosophers* (Cambridge, MA: Harvard UP).

'the cold is a bond': Archelāus of Athens (same source).

Orphic fragments inform the last sections (same source).

Vitruvian Shadows:

All words in italics are from Vitruvius, *The Ten Books on Architecture*, tr Morris Hickey Morgan, NY: Dover, (1914) 1960.

The very last line of the poem sequence refers to James Joyce's *Ulysses*.

In the piece for Diane Arbus, the quotation "Measured outlines, like footprints, have no point of view" is taken from Massimo Scolari, *Oblique Drawing: A History of Anti-Perspective*.

If you feel you've recognised a quotation or paraphrase I haven't mentioned, you're most probably right.

– David Miller

David Miller

David Miller's recent publications include *Reassembling Still: Collected Poems* (Shearsman, 2014), *Spiritual Letters* (Contraband Books, 2017), *Towards a Menagerie* (Chax Press, 2019), *Matrix I & II* (Guillemot Press, 2020) and *Some Other Days and Nights* (above/ground press, 2021). He has compiled *British Poetry Magazines 1914-2000: A History and Bibliography of 'Little Magazines'* (with Richard Price, The British Library / Oak Knoll Press, 2006) and edited *The Lariat and Other Writings by Jaime de Angulo* (Counterpoint, 2009) and *The Alchemist's Mind: a book of narrative prose by poets* (Reality Street, 2012). He is also a musician and a member of the Frog Peak Music collective, and has performed and recorded as part of The Mind Shop and with Louise Landes Levi, Ken White, Rod Boucher and others. Previous books and chapbooks have appeared from Enitharmon, Gaberbocchus, Arc, Stride, Reality Street, Burning Deck, Singing Horse, Chax, hawkhaven and Harbor Mountain. Originally from Australia, he currently lives in London and Bridport, Dorset.